# TRACTION ENGINES
## in Colour

Fowler showmans engine No 20223 *Supreme*, registration number EU 5313, built 1934, 10nhp, DDC, Class B6.

# TRACTION ENGINES
## in Colour

**BARRY J. FINCH** AIIP

LONDON
IAN ALLAN LTD

First published 1980

ISBN 0 7110 1032 3



© Barry J. Finch 1980

Published by Ian Allan Ltd, Shepperton, Surrey; and printed by Ian Allan Printing Ltd at their works at Coombelands in Runnymede, England

*Front cover:* Like most traction engine builders, E. Foden Sons and Company Limited (better known merely as Fodens Limited) were founded over a century ago in 1856. Unlike most of the others however, Fodens are still in existence manufacturing fine self-propelled vehicles.

Fodens have, of course, become famous for their heavy lorries, steam for many years, but nowadays diesel-engined. Many of their steam wagons are still in existence and are a fairly common sight at rallies (a photograph of a fine example appears elsewhere in this book). But in the early days Fodens were active in the agricultural field producing traction engines and the equipment that went with them; this ceased more or less about the start of World War I in 1914 when work was concentrated on the steam wagon.

Few of their traction engines exist today, but here is a photograph of a fine example, works number 3384, which was built in 1912. This is a compound engine, ie one using the steam twice in two cylinders — the steam passing from one to the other to take advantage of expansion of the steam. It is of 7nhp; the two cylinder ends can clearly be seen.

The road registration number is SN 1646, indicating Scottish ownership; Adams Bros of Dumbarton were first owners. It bears the name *Wattie Pollock.*

*Back cover:* There are several illustrations in this book of the true agricultural traction engine, which, generally speaking, did not differ greatly in appearance from make to make. A few of the photographs are of a traction engine carrying out its main duty of threshing out corn. Before the days of the combine harvester the traction engine was the main source of power to drive the threshing drum and ancillary equipment.

This photograph shows a typical agricultural view as it might have been at many a farm or stackyard, although it was taken at what is usually termed a 'working rally'. But the Fowler engine works number 15710 has been doing a real job.

Some manufacturers classified their products; John Fowler & Company (Leeds) Limited, was one such and number 15710 is a Class A9 engine of 7nhp, which was built in December 1922 and sold new to Mr D. Sharpe of Faringdon, Berkshire. Hence it carries the Berkshire road registration number MO 780. This engine also has the name *Tommy* said to be after its first driver. The angle of this photograph gives a good view of the footplate and controls.

This engine has spent all its life in Berkshire and is at present owned by Mr Arthur Napper whose traction engine races in 1950 with a neighbouring farmer sparked off the present preservation movement.

# Introduction

My interest in photography began as a schoolboy but by my late teenage years I felt very proud occasionally to have a picture published and flattered to be asked to take on many different types of photographic commisssions.

It was my eldest brother who introduced me to traction engines when he asked me to take a series of pictures of a Davey Paxman agricultural engine, in great detail, to accompany his drawings from which he planned to make a working model.

This work I found both fascinating and rewarding. The patterns made by the sun on the spokes, safety valves, governors, etc, were a joy to capture in pictures. The time spent climbing over the engine, the people I met who worked in the yard and all the talk I heard about other engines was to be the beginning of an interest that has sent me round the country taking photographs, trying each time to obtain better pictures than I had before of more and more types of engines, and meeting more of the friendly people connected with them.

These were the days before the now familiar rallies; the days when the engines which were in working condition, and indeed that were still at work, mostly seemed to appear the same colour until the mixture of dust and oil was wiped away with a paraffin soaked rag or the mud removed from the massive wheels with a water hose.

Then, and only then, could you see the colour that had been applied so many years before, often the original paint put on by the manufacturer.

To photograph the engines I would have to travel many miles. There was a terrific sense of satisfaction to be found in locating a pair of Fowler ploughing engines that I had been told were out at work in Hertfordshire and Essex, or a steam roller in Kent or Surrey. On other occasions there were 'steam ups' by individual owners on their own land sometimes accompanied by a short road run round the village green. To see an engine in steam on the move was to me a dream come true. I could now take several photographs of the same engine with different backgrounds, although looking back at some of my earlier pictures they often seem to have a telegraph pole growing from their chimneys!

The late John Patten of Little Hadham in Hertfordshire, whose sets of ploughing engines had for years been seen at work in the surrounding countryside or on the move along the country lanes with all their tackle, must be the owner whose name first comes to my mind. I spent many happy days watching his engines often when the weather was so bad the idea of taking photographs was unthinkable. Chris Lambert of Horsmonden in Kent was another owner who allowed me to spend many days in his yard taking pictures of his engines, mainly traction engines and rollers. Over the years his private 'steam days' gradually attracted more and more spectators and

*Left:* One of the author's earliest traction engine detail photographs.

*Right:* Outside the 'California' pub in Belmont, near Sutton, local transport enthusiasts inspect a small exhibition for charity. Traction engines are often in demand for this sort of public appearance and command large appreciative audiences.

WATNEYS
THE FAIRGROUND SOCIETY
BURRELL
W. HARDWICK & SONS.

Mr R. Winsford's model Garrett, showing the superb detail and novel method of driving!

McLaren agricultural traction engine No 547
(registration number BD 5448, built 1896, 6nhp,
two speed) followed by Aveling & Porter road
roller No 5541 *Bo-Peep*.

enthusiasts from all over the country and must be considered the forerunners of the
traction engine rally as we know it today.

Ben Taylor of Wimbish, who alas died recently, is yet another whose name will be
remembered and talked of for many years to come, especially by those whose interest
in steam is particularly towards steam ploughing and cultivating. By the time this
book is published the sale of his engines will have taken place. This must be the last
such sale of a complete set of steam plough tackle to have been seen working so
recently.

A large ploughing engine built by John Fowler of Leeds. Note the winding drum under the boiler.

These three men are but a few of the many that I have met — there are many others who, because of their love for the steam engines they worked and because of their own enthusiasm and personalities, did so much, probably quite without being aware of it themselves, to further interest in steam engines. This interest led to the formation of a movement that today organises the rallies, steam fairs and the many varied appearances of all types of steam engines for the pleasure of hundreds of thousands of spectators every year.

The people who have been and are connected with the many clubs throughout the country have done so much to preserve the engines, and in many cases to restore them to their original condition and livery, that my hopes of one day having a photograph of every existing engine in the country have long since been shattered — I just could not keep up!

However, the work the owners have lavished on their engines has encouraged me to put together a selection of coloured pictures that I hope will give some pleasure to many who like myself appreciate the skill and care the owners show, but never cease to wonder just how they achieve such perfection with engines that perhaps only relatively few years ago were red with rust.

During the growth of the popularity of the steam rallies many owners have willingly assisted me by positioning their engines in accordance with my requests to enable me to photograph them. To them I say a big 'thank you'; I only wish I had been able to include all the pictures in this book. I would also like to take this opportunity to thank everyone else who has helped me so much in many different ways and hope that in the years to come I will meet many more enthusiasts and take many more pictures that may one day make up another book that will at least bring some enjoyment to those who are unable to travel to see the traction engines themselves.

*B. J. Finch*

Wallington, Surrey                                                       June 1980

*Left:* Fowler agricultural engine No 8224 *Mary*; registration number HK 9982, built 1894, 8nph.

*Above:* A pair of Fowler ploughing engines at work in the mid-1950s. Note 'living van' at right where the workers lived during the working period.

OWNERS WEST OF ENGLAND    STEAM ENGINE SOCIETY
TA 1063

*Left:* An Aveling & Porter steam tractor which has had the canopy as a later addition.

*Overleaf, left:* Wallis & Steevens traction engine No 7801, registration number PU 3378, built 1924, single-cylinder.

*Overleaf, right:* The prime activity of work for an agricultural traction engine was to drive a threshing drum. It is nice to see an engine with the equipment it was made to work with — somehow it does not seem 'right' without it. The threshing drum itself was an interesting and highly complicated machine; although there are some preserved, it seems a pity that more are not maintained by traction engine owners to form the 'full scene'.

Driving the drum was by means of a belt, from the engine flywheel to a pulley wheel on the side of the drum; this can be clearly seen in this photograph. A number of small belts and pulleys were also used on different parts of the drum itself and some of these can be seen as well.

The engine is this photograph was made by Wallis & Steevens Limited of Basingstoke and is a single cylinder engine of 7nhp, with the works number 7102. It was built in July 1909 and was new to Mr J. Meakins of Edlesborough, near Dunstable. Subsequently it moved to Buckinghamshire where it received the road registration number, BH 7446, under the requirements of the Finance Act, 1920. It is now in Dorset and carries the name *The Reeder Express.*

*Overleaf, left:* Davey Paxman & Company Limited of Standard Ironworks, Colchester need no
introduction as engineers — they have a long history and are still in existence today. Their products are
wellknown and their engines world famous.

They entered the traction engine field later than some manufacturers, and although they produced a
range of different types very few of their engines exist today — all that do are traction engines. A well
cared for example from the last batch of traction engines they made to a War Department order in
1916 is shown here.

A traction engine of 7nhp with works number 19412, displaying all the typical agricultural traction
engine features; single cylinder with slide valves (the valve cover can be clearly seen on the side  of the
cylinder blook), spoked flywheel and iron shod wheels.

Two features are worth noting. First the steering on the nearside from the simple steering wheel, the
rod to the final chain to each end of the front axle; traction engines with a few exceptions use this type
of steering. The other is the inspection cover on the side of the boiler just in front of the flywheel.

The road registration number KE 2700, suggests Kentish ownership and indeed, this engine has
spent most of its life there with quite a few owners including, for a short time, a relative of the author.

*Overleaf, right:* Marshall, Sons & Company Limited, probably produced as much agricultural
equipment as any other manufacturer in England. Many and varied were their products and the range
naturally included the agricultural traction engine.

The true traction engine, as opposed to the more general use of the term, was designed and built for
agricultural purposes which would include all manner of farm duties, many driving machinery on the
belt from the flywheel.

Usually the engines were of two speeds only permitting, say, 3 and 6mph if used on the road and
were frequently unsprung engines (although springing could be and frequently was included if desired).
An agricultural engine can be identified by the spoked flywheel.

This illustration shows a typical Marshall traction engine; it is makers number 55437, built in
December 1910 and is of 6nhp and single cylinder.

The first owners were Messrs D. A. Fyfe & Co, of Littleport, Cambridgeshire — hence the
Cambridge registration number EB 2873. Subsequently it had other owners in the eastern counties
before it went to the Thames Valley area where it is still to be seen at rallies.

The ex-farm tractor rubber tyres on the rear wheels are a later addition.

EB 2873

*Overleaf, left:* The agricultural traction engine was manufactured over a fairly long period, stretching
from the 1860s to as late as the 1930s — a 75-year span. Any engine built before 1900 can claim to be
a veteran among veterans; the Burrell shown comes within this category and is a fine early specimen
built in June 1895 which bears the makers number 1840.

The earlier type engines frequently had a much shorter smokebox and this is plainly visible in this
picture — compare it with some of the photographs of later engines. Of note also is the name of the
maker and the town of manufacture, embossed on the slide valve cover, not a separate plate as in later
engines.

This is a typical single cylinder engine of the period and is rated at 6nhp. When it was new it was
exhibited at Taunton Show and the earliest known owners were B. & J. C. Mitchell of Merriott,
Somerset. Later it was owned by Mr P. W. Cole also of Somerset; and was still in that county in 1920
when it received the road registration number YA 2481. The present name of *Duke of Windsor* is, of
course, a more recent addition; names for traction engines being almost unheard of in their working
days (at least officially with brass nameplates) although no doubt they were given pet names by their
crews from time to time!

*Overleaf, right:* Mention is made elsewhere in this book that the majority of the traction engine
manufacturers were in eastern England — with the exception of that great steam engine construction
centre of Leeds, of which more is written elsewhere.

But there were many smaller builders of traction engines in various parts of the country, some of
which were sizeable in their own way, although they tended to deal locally and serve a more limited
area. A number of such small builders were in the mid south-west of England. Messrs Robinson &
Auden of Wantage, Berkshire, were one such, later being known as the Wantage Engineering
Company.

Several of their steam engines survive to this day, but you will have to look hard to find them. A fine
example is shown here. Robinson & Auden number 1376 of 6nhp is a good example of a plain but solid
traction engine. It exhibits all the features of an agricultural engine but of particular interest is the fine
cast plate on the slide valve cover of the cylinder giving all the information about the engine, viz
'Robinson & Auden Ltd. Engineers, Wantage. No 1376 6 HP'.

It carries the road registration number AD 8889, its first owners being Messrs Hulcke, Comery &
Co, of Gloucester. This engine was built in 1889.

EV 6560
KING GEORGE V
THE BURRELL
TRACTION ENGINE

*Overleaf, left:* Messrs Charles Burrell & Sons Limited of Thetford, Norfolk, made their first self-propelled road steam engine in 1856 and their last in 1932 (actually assembled at Garretts of Leiston). During this time many and various types were made and it is fortunate that fairly comprehensive records of this manufacturer exist, so that we can obtain quite a lot of data about any particular engine.

Having said this, the picture presents one of the few mystery engines. What can be said with certainty is that it is a fine, and probably quite old engine.

Certain features are of particular note; like the other early Burrell traction engine *Duke of Windsor* it has the short smokebox of early engines, but the smokebox door does not have any adornment. This engine also has the earlier type Salter safety valves which were in vogue in the 1870s and 1880s, so it could well date from this period.

One certain identification is the registration number CF 3667, which indicates it was in west Suffolk in or just after 1920 a fact borne out by its ownership by W. J. Ford & Sons of Mildenhall for many years. Whilst some traction engines move considerable distances with change of ownership, this one has not been so venturesome and is still in Suffolk at the time of writing.

*Overleaf, right:* Elsewhere in this book is a photograph of a typical traction engine built by Clayton & Shuttleworth Limited at the Stamp End Works, Lincoln. Here is another one.

The eastern counties of England, being drier and flatter than those in the west, are essentially arable areas. Arable land demands much machinery and with this demand, the firms to supply the machinery came into being and prospered. Nearly all the traction engine builders were on the eastern side of the country and several were in Lincoln.

Clayton & Shuttleworth were one such manufacturer and this example of their products is still in the county. Bearing the works number 47015, it is a single cylinder engine of 7nhp (this power rating is almost the standard for single cylinder traction engines).

This engine was supplied new to Mr S. Jones of Wollaston, Wellingborough, Northants who would most probably still have had the engine in the early 1920s when it received the Northamptonshire road registration number BD 5483.

But this engine carries another number — a small round plate reading 'Northants C.C. No 238'. This is a form of registration or licence to take the engine on the public highway and issued in accordance with the Locomotive Act of 1898 (which was superseded by the Finance Act, 1920, enforcing road registration for those vehicles not already registered). It is worth while looking for these small round plates on older agricultural engines.

*Left:* Marshall traction engine No 54587 *Pride of the Road.* Registration number AJ 5781, built 1910, 10.5ton, single-cylinder.

*Overleaf, left:* Marshall, Sons & Company Limited of Gainsborough, manufacturerd many products for the agricultural industry, including many traction engines and associated equipment.

This photograph shows a typical Marshall traction engine driving a threshing drum (although it was not actually working when the view was taken).

This particular engine is works number 52367, built in 1909 and of 7nhp and a single cylinder with slide valve. This was the 'standard' Marshall traction engine which was of rugged but simple construction. That they stood the test of time is evident by the considerable number of this type which are still in existence today.

The first owner was Mr J. Wilkerson of Wybaston, Bedford and the engine has had only three owners in its lifetime and is still in north Buckinghamshire.

The 1920 Finance Act required all vehicles that used the road at any time and not already registered to do so forthwith; so number 52367 received the road registration number NM 182 of Bedfordshire about this time.

Of particular note is how the engine is set to the threshing drum — it was most important that the pulleys and flywheel were correctly lined up or the belt might fly off. Setting is not so easy as it looks and even more difficult in a cramped and sloping stackyard where blocks had frequently to be used.

*Overleaf, right:* Mention has been made elsewhere in this book of how many traction engine manufacturers were situated on the eastern, arable, side of England. Ruston, Proctor and Company of the Sheaf Iron Works, Lincoln, are yet another example of this.

Serving an agricultural community and making all manner of machinery and equipment for farmers, it is only natural that the agricultural traction engine should be among their products. The first were probably produced by the mid-1870s and although never made in great numbers, they were nevertheless fine machines. It is interesting to note the following from their catalogue of the early 1900s: 'Our traction engines are specially adapted for agricultural purposes, the working parts are of great strength, conveniently arranged so as to secure the utmost efficiency, durability and simplicity, with economy in fuel'. So advertising has not changed.

This photograph shows works number 50278, of 7nhp built in 1914, makers class SHS and new to C. R. Pumfrey & Sons of Cambridgeshire, by which family the engine is still owned. What a fine record! This engine has another record too; that of baling 242 tons of hay in one week during World War I. So it is aptly named *Success.* It carries the Cambridgeshire road registration number CE 7949, and also a Locomotive Act plate 'Cambridge C.C. 304'.

NM 182

B. & E. BOURN, DEDHAM.
GAY GIRL.

*Left:* Burrell agricultural traction engine No 3474 *Gay Girl*. Registration number SP 5348, built 1913, 8nhp, SCC, three speed, photographed at Kelvedon.

*Overleaf, left:* Clayton and Shuttleworth Limited of Stamp End Works, Lincoln, were amongst the earliest of portable and self-moving steam engine builders; the partnership between the founders whose names the company bears being entered into in 1842. The company lasted with some changes in constitution until absorbed into Marshall, Sons & Company Limited of Gainsborough in 1929.

During this time they turned out great quantities of mechanical equipment of all kinds, although most of it was agricultural machinery including large numbers of portable and self-moving steam engines.

This photograph is of a typical agricultural traction engine made by Clayton and Shuttleworth. Single cylinder and of 7nph, number 36336, built in 1904, appears regularly at rallies in south-east England and carries the name *Peggy*.

The traction engine often encountered soft ground in its agricultural duties and the ridges on the rear wheels, known as strakes, which gave a good grip, can be clearly seen. These strakes were usually set at an angle so that the edge nearest to the engine met the ground first. If conditions proved too soft or slippery for the wheels, extension bars could be fitted on — this photograph shows clearly the set of these between the wheels and also the holes in the rear wheel for fitting.

This engine carries the road registration number BP 5821.

*Overleaf, right:* Mention is made elsewhere in these descriptive notes of the equipment that is associated with traction engines. Their most usual duty was to drive a threshing drum and to haul it and other items that made up the complete set from place to place as required.

But traction engines being a mobile source of power were readily adaptable to other duties. One of these was to drive a saw bench using a belt off the flywheel in similar fashion to driving a drum. The engine in this photograph is doing just this, although it is a pity the saw bench cannot be seen. They were fearsome looking pieces of equipment with a large, usually unguarded, circular saw on the saw table. Saw benches often appear at working rallies — look out for one; they are very interesting.

The fine proportions and good looks of the Burrell traction engine are shown to advantage in this photograph of number 3984, which is another makers version of the almost standard 7nhp engine. This engine was made in August 1924 and bears the road registration number NU 4495, and is named *Dolly*. The present owner has a timber trailer to go with the engine.

CLAYTON AND SHUTTLEWORTH LTD
LINCOLN
BP 5821

G F A GILBERT & SON
NORTHCHURCH HERTS
NU4495

R. H. JENNINGS,    BISSOE
AF 3520
COUNTESS
R.W.HAYNE

*Overleaf, left:* Other photographs appear in this book of engines built by Marshall, Sons and Company Limited of Gainsborough, Lincolnshire. This photograph depicts one of their products in what might be termed the 'middle' period of traction engine building.

The eastern counties of England being largely arable land produced many small engineering works, mainly devoted to manufacturing and repairing implements and equipment for farmers. Marshalls were one such firm. The founder was William Marshall who went into business in Gainsborough in 1842. The firm grew rapidly and their premises became known as the Britannia Iron Works.

Their first traction engine was produced in the mid-1870s and production of these basic agricultural types continued until the 1930s, with development all the time; the final versions were excellent engines with all the trimmings.

Marshall engines were always popular with farmers and many examples — usually single cylinder types — are in existence today. This photograph shows a typical single cylinder, 7nhp traction engine built in July 1913 with the works number 61970, and the road registration number BJ 5934.

It has had a varied history with a long period in a scrapyard at Fakenham and was also owned for a while by Mr Palmer of West Dereham, also in Norfolk. The solid rubber tyres were fitted in preservation days to facilitate movement by road.

*Overleaf, right:* East Anglia must hold the record for old established firms giving service over many years to the agricultural community. Agriculture has always demanded a skilful and imaginative back-up service industry to supply it with its 'tools of the trade' — and, of course, still does today.

Garretts of Leiston have been mentioned elsewhere in this book and now it is the turn of another Suffolk firm, probably even better known — Ransomes, Sims & Jefferies Limited of Orwell Works, Ipswich.

The original Robert Ransome set up business in Ipswich in 1789 undertaking general foundry work, but concentrating on ploughshares and lawn-mowers, for both of which they became world famous.

In the 1850s they produced their first self-moving steam engine and the type for agricultural use continued to be developed and produced into the 1930s in the usual full range of sizes.

This photograph shows a later type of compound traction engine built in 1926 and bearing works number 37087. The compound version of agricultural engines was never so numerous as the single cylinder type, but was claimed to be more economical. This engine is of 6nhp has slide valves mounted on the side of each cylinder. It is also 'spring mounted' so that it could be regarded more as a general purpose engine. The road registration number is FP 1754 of Rutland and its first owners were Messrs Harris & Goodwin of Ingthorpe.

BJ5934

PW 8905

*Left:* Burrell traction engine No 4048 *William the Second*, registration number PW 8905, built 1926, single-cylinder, photographed at Haslemere 1970.

*Overleaf, left:* The words 'traction engine' can be used in a general sense to indicate all engines of a generally similar outline, but within the general category comes the road engine, which is an engine specifically built to run on a road with general haulage in mind. Hence the specification of a road engine included many features not necessarily required in an engine designed for agricultural use.

When an engine went on a road journey water supplies could become a problem as this usually had to be drawn from wayside streams, ponds or rivers en route, almost all engines being equipped to pick up or 'lift' water. In order to give a road engine a greater range between pick-ups than the normal water tank under the tender could provide, it was usual to fit additional tanks under and each side of the boiler known as 'belly tanks'. These are easily seen in this photograph and are a feature which will be seen in several other pictures.

The makers number is 3824, and this engine was built in December 1919 and sold to its first owners — A Shire & Sons of Thurlbear — in 1920. It is of 5nhp and has the registration number YA 366. Of particular interest is the fact that this engine is fitted with governors and the road weight on the perch bracket below the smokebox can be clearly seen. This engine has the name *Lord Fisher of Lambeth*.

*Overleaf, right:* Charles Burrell & Sons Limited manufactured all types of self-propelled steam engines, amongst which were many fine road engines. Here is a good example of this type without a canopy or cab and so looking very much as most Burrell road engines did when built and when in use.

Burrell number 2824 was built in June 1906 and is a fairly early example of a road engine. It is fitted with solid rubber tyres (still obtainable at a price) which were an addition to the engine long after it was built. As the surfaces of roads were gradually improved, so the tread of the wheels on road using vehicles were improved to cause less wear to both — a feature sometimes helped by legislation from time to time.

This engine started its life at Neston in the Wirral Peninsula and was owned by R. Bridson & Sons, a firm who used steam until quite recently. By 1915 it was owned by the Eddison Steam Rolling Company of Dorchester and later by Messrs Chivers of Devizes, Wiltshire, when it acquired its Wiltshire number of HR 4142. It lay derelict for many years near Romsey and continued its move east to be brought back into full working order and preservation in Sussex. It is of 7nhp and is spring mounted and has the name *Lord Lansdowne*.

THE "BURRELL" ROAD LOCOMOTIVE — BUILT 1920
YA 366
Lord Fisher of Lambeth

HD 4142

*Left:* Built in 1919 this ploughing engine by Mc Laren (makers number 1552) was named *Hero* and was one of the only two such large machines made by this Leeds firm. Note the large winding drum under the boiler, which has been taken from a Fowler engine and converted. The weight of this engine in working order is 22ton.

*Overleaf, left:* This book contains a variety of the traction engine products of Marshall, Sons & Company Limited of Gainsborough, and this photograph is of particular interest. Marshalls never built road engines to the extent that some manufacturers did, concentrating primarily on the agricultural and road rolling field.

However, the engine shown here is a road engine or as near as Marshalls usually got to one; sometimes this might be called a general purpose engine. Number 57304 with the name *Challenger* has the appearance of a traction engine and is equipped with governors, so it could be used for belt work. Nevertheless it is a compound, three speed engine with solid flywheel and fully sprung so it was intended for use on the road. The 7nhp is sufficient for either road or agricultural work. Incidentally the ring on the smokebox door announces it to be 'Marshalls Compound Traction'.

It was built in 1911 and was new to Mr G. D. Lucas of Shinfield, Berkshire. Later it was owned by Messrs W. Reynolds of Bedford, who had many engines in the course of time and must have been there in 1921 to receive the Bedfordshire road registration number TM 4430. It moved to Essex before making for Hampshire where it is now in preservation and appearing regularly at rallies.

*Overleaf, right:* There were two main applications to agriculture of the self-moving steam traction engine. This book contains several illustrations of the true agricultural traction engine, whose main duty was as a mobile power plant used to drive the machinery in question by a belt from the flywheel, and to move the equipment from place to place.

The second main application was to cultivate the land. Many and various were the early experiments but the use of steam power in this context was established by the 1850s; what eventually became the most widely used and successful system — the double engine system — was in operation by 1865.

Few ploughing engines and even less equipment are still in existence today from those early times; possibly about 10 engines built before 1880 survive, not all in working order. Most of those about the rally fields have been rebuilt during their long existence with parts supplied by the Oxford Steam Ploughing Co Limited. Two illustrations of such engines are in this book.

Built 1874, number AL 8344 is an excellent example of an 'early 14' or, maybe 'late 14' single cylinder ploughing engine built by John Fowler & Company (Leeds) Limited shown here with a cultivator. Note particularly the winding drum under the boiler and the guiding pulley wheels through which the wire rope passes and the small plate on the smokebox door reading '12 tons' — I wonder!

AL 8344

NO 373

*Left:* Fowler ploughing engine No 15563. Registration number NO 373, built 1920, 18nhp Class AA7.

*Overleaf, left:* John Fowler & Company (Leeds) Limited, in a catalogue published about 1906, state: 'Since the year 1850 we have been continually manufacturing and perfecting machinery required in connection with cultivation of the soil'. Whilst there are no engines still extant from those very early days there are a few from the early 1870s — of which two photographs appear in this book. In general design and detail they are similar, so the remarks regarding number AL 8463 and this page apply to a large extent to number AL 8344.

Ploughing engines, as they came to be known after their most usual operation of working a cable hauled plough, being agricultural engines were dealt with under the Locomotive Act of 1898 and were registered by the appropriate county authority and a small plate issued; some ploughing engines still carry these early plates. Subsequently they received a normal road registration and the AL gives their common earlier habitat of Nottinghamshire. In fact both engines were owned for many years by Messrs Beeby of Rempstone and almost certainly before that by Messrs Angrave and Burrows.

This engine which is said to date from 1872 and probably carried the makers number 2013, was rebuilt by Messrs Beeby with Oxford Steam Ploughing Company parts in 1916; the long smokebox with handsome flared chimney and double internal spring safety valves give the typical Oxford appearance.

The engine is named *Noreen* and is well known in the Thames Valley area with its partner *Margaret.*

*Overleaf, right:* Although other manufacturers built ploughing engines of various types John Fowler & Company (Leeds) Limited turned out far more of this type than all others put together; no wonder their works were called the 'Steam Plough & Locomotive Works'.

The general principle of the double engine system of steam cultivation — which became almost universally adopted — was for an engine to stand on each headland (at each side of the field). The implement to be used or worked was attached to the wire rope on the drum, clearly seen under the engine boiler in the photograph. Each engine winched the implement across the field in turn, and moved up a short distance when the opposite engine was pulling. Thus the whole field was gradually dealt with as the engines moved up the headlands with the implement moving backwards and forwards.

This is a fine example of a Fowler compound ploughing engine built in 1920 with the works number 15441. It has the Lincolnshire (Kesteven) road registration number CT 4177, and has spent most of its life in the same county, being new to Mr T. H. Richardson of Keisby and later owned by Mr H. H. Gurnhill of Saxilby. It is of makers Class BB1 — 16nhp with the fine name of *Lion* (its sister engine is *Tiger*).

NOREEN
1872
AL 8463

FRED COUPLAND
STEAM PLOUGHING
CONTRACTOR
GT 4177

*Left:* A typical steam roller of Marshall manufacture.

*Overleaf, left:* Many of the photographs in this book are of traction engines made expressly to run and earn their keep on the road. But how did the smooth, hard road required by these engines get there? Up to the middle of the 19th century roads had been constructed largely by throwing down stones of various sizes and leaving the traffic to level if off in due course.

Then came the steam road roller that was to revolutionise the road making industry. This was really a traction engine with rolls in place of the wheels — a large single roll in front with two narrower ones at the back. When Thomas Aveling built the first steam roller in 1867 it started this general pattern that has been followed ever since (with a few diversions into other designs).

Aveling and Porter Limited of Rochester built thousands of steam rollers and this photograph shows a good example. It is works number 10596 built in 1923 and of 10 tons weight (rollers are usually identified by their weight) and is of Class E. It was delivered new to Messrs W. W. Buncombe of Highbridge, Somerset — a large road rolling contractor whose plate is still on the motion covers with the fleet number 41 on the headstock.

The road registration is number YA 5385, of Somerset County. Note also the Aveling & Porter scarifier mounted on the rear, this incorporated the 'Price' patent which had a spring-loaded shock absorber and was a 'single direction' scarifier.

*Overleaf, right:* The firm of Marshall, Sons and Company Limited have been in existence for a great many years, producing at their Britannia Iron Works, Gainsborough, all manner of agricultural machinery.

Road rollers have formed a large part of their production in later years and are, of course, still being produced there.

This photograph shows a fine well preserved specimen of their later steam rollers. This is makers number 86104 which was built in 1931, is of 8 tons, and driven by a single cylinder slide valve engine. It carries the Lincolnshire (Lindsey) road registration number FW 2355.

It was delivered new to Messrs G. Roberts and Sons of Caistor and moved subsequently to the Doncaster area before returning to Lincolnshire near to where it was built.

The typical round Marshall headstock above the front roll is easily seen, as are the deep motion covers on the side. The scarifier with which most rollers were fitted in their working days is clearly seen attached to the nearside rear axle with the hand wheel used by the operator to raise or lower the tines used to break up the road surface or hardcore underneath.

Nº 41
YA 5385

*Overleaf, left:* Most of the traction engine manufacturers built steam road rollers, and it is interesting to reflect that the term 'steam roller' is still in fairly common use today although you would have to look a long way before you found a 'steam' roller in commercial use.

The firm of Aveling and Porter of Rochester were amongst the earliest of traction engine makers and are still in existence today, although no longer in Kent and with name slightly changed. But Avelings still build road rollers and the prancing horse 'Invicta' symbol, seen to advantage in this photograph, is quite well known and often seen.

Local and county councils as the authorities responsible for the upkeep of the roads, were extensive owners of steam rollers.

This photograph shows a late example of the long Aveling line, being number 12103 built in 1928 of 10 tons and supplied new to Dumfries County Council whose plate still adorns the motion cover; it carries the appropriate Dumfrieshire road registration number SM 7013. The engine is single cylinder and piston valve as can be clearly seen in this view and is of Class E. It has now come south and has had several owners and is fairly well known in the Surrey, Sussex area.

*Overleaf, right:* The steam roller occupies a very special place in the history of powered transport on the road for it was used to make the road — the firm hard tarmac surface that we know today is evolved from the first steam rolled roads. In early days most roads were made by layers of stones — large at the bottom, smaller on top; each layer rolled well down with sand or grit on top. All this laying and rolling being accompanied by watering, so this process became known as 'water-bound' roads. Later, of course, concrete and tarmac were introduced.

Nearly every maker turned out steam rollers at some time or another; a great number were from the Steam Plough Works of John Fowler & Company (Leeds) Limited — this photograph is a fine example in preservation of one of their products — a late one in fact, with the works number 18625, which was turned out in 1929. Steam rollers were always known by their weight and this one is '8 tons'.

The points to note are the scarifier behind the rear roll, the water lift pipe and the roll and chain steering. The scraper by the front of the rear roll is also visible. The road registration number is TK 4285 and it is a single cylinder engine.

SM 7013

A.W. FIELD "Fippenny Queen"
TK 4285
FOWLER
A W FIELD

PG 9014

*Left:* This Aveling & Porter steam roller was a common sight on roads throughout the country in the 1920s/1930s.

*Overleaf, left:* Taskers of Andover have been in existence for very many years, producing during this time a great variety of agricultural implements, most of the parts being cast in their own foundry and finished at the Anna Valley Works. The original Mr Tasker was a blacksmith.

During this long existence they made quite a number of traction engines of various types but became latterly well known for the smaller type of road engine usually known as a steam (motor) tractor. These engines came within the Motor Car Act of 1903 or, more particularly, the 1904 Extension to the 1903 Act, which was an Order in Council, not an Act in itself and covered three and five ton steam Motor tractors and steam wagons (it also concerned other matters).

From the steam tractor was developed the steam roller, basically a similar engine except for the substitution of rolls for wheels. Sometimes these were produced as convertibles with sets of wheels and rolls enabling the owners — often local authorities — to use them in either haulage or rolling.

This illustration is of an engine originally exhibited at the Royal Show in 1909 and sold to W. H. Snook of Yeovil as a tractor. Later it had owners in Chippenham and Swindon and spent some time in the Tasker Museum. It has the makers number 1409 and road registration number AA2299 and a weight of 8 tons.

*Overleaf, right:* During the many years that Charles Burrell & Sons were manufacturing traction engines at Thetford, most types were built at one time or another. Many steam road rollers were turned out and this is a good example of one, built before World War 1 in October 1908.

Number 3047 was '10 tons' (rollers usually being classified by their weight rather than nominal horsepower) and was fitted with a scarifier for tearing up the road surface. This was normally fitted on the offside rear axle and so is not visible in this photograph.

This engine was delivered new to T. R. Doran, a contractor of Thetford who operated a number of Burrell rollers. It has spent all its life in the eastern counties and its present owner is Mr Burgess, who has been responsible for much fine renovation and engineering work on engines now in preservation — a photograph of his fine show engine *Earl Haig* is included in this book.

Burrell engines are generally considered to be good-looking engines with finely proportioned lines, this feature is well illustrated in this photograph. This engine carries the road registration number AH 6867.

BUILT
1909
LITTLE GIANT
AA 2299
G. JESSETT
WHADLOW DOWN

S.A.BURGESS & SONS
S.A.BURGESS & SONS,
ENGINEERS,
HADDENHAM, CAMBS.

R. H. JE
AH 648

*Left:* A Fowler engine now beautifully preserved.

*Overleaf, left:* In some ways this photograph is of an engine that is an 'odd-man-out'. At first sight it might appear to be a conventional steam roller; and so it is. But the difference is that whereas every other engine in this book was made in England, this one was not. In fact it is a product of the German firm of Zettelmeyer.

It was never used in this country commercially, and is a preservation item. How it came to be here at all makes an interesting story. Mr Leslie Birch of Sellinge in Kent was on holiday in France at the town of Gurat; there is a fair-sized contractors yard in the town and Mr Birch, being a contractor himself, naturally took an interest in the equipment in the yard. He noticed this steam roller, took a fancy to it and was eventually able to purchase it after protracted negotiation lasting over two years.

It is a fairly heavy machine weighing 15 tons and is about 6nhp. It also incorporates a single crank compound engine — that is two cylinders but only one crank incorporating a large crosshead with two piston rods — to save weight and moving parts. This system of compounding was much favoured by Burrells in earlier years.

Now fully overhauled by Mr Birch, this roller is well-known in south-east England; it bears the works number 553 and was built in 1930.

*Overleaf, right:* Although most manufacturers built road engines at various times, in the latter period of building most of this type were turned out by John Fowler & Company (Leeds) Limited. The largest class they built in any numbers for home use was the Class B6, several examples of which exist today, some in the showland form adorned with dynamo, twisted brass etc, usually associated with engines used by travelling amusement caterers.

This photograph shows a Fowler Class B6 in the crane engine form. This particular engine has the works number 17106, and was built at the Leeds works in 1928 and bears the proud name *Duke of York*. The road registration number KD 2826, indicates it was new to a Liverpool owner. At one time it was in the fleet of Edward Box Limited of Liverpool; this is a name much associated with heavy road transport and many photographs exist of the big Fowlers at work.

Some idea of the size of the engine can be gauged by comparing it with the truck in the background whilst details of the drive for the crane are visible. Note also the water lift pipe attached to the belly tank — the bottom end would be put into a convenient pond or stream to lift water when the tanks required replenishment.

ZETTELMEYER    CONZ b. TRIER

XD 2826
KD 2826

PRINCESS MARY
NO 8287

*Left:* This Burrell double cranked compound showmans road locomotive (makers number 3949) weighs 17ton, has three speeds and was built in 1923. It was originally owned by W. Nicolls who then had their headquarters at Forest Gate, East London. They later sold it to another showman, C. Presland & Sons of Tilbury, who used it on fairgrounds until 1958; thus this is believed to be the last Burrell in regular active service. It is named *Princess Mary.*

*Overleaf, left:* Firms who manufacture heavy plant and machinery have recourse to move these items in their works; when completed these items have to be moved again either to the customer or, maybe, to docks for shipment. Mobile cranes and heavy road tractors take a large part in this movement. Before the days of the all-conquering diesel engine, steam played its part in such operations.

This brings us to photographs of that most magnificent of all traction engines — the steam crane road engine. Crane engines — that is engines which had a jib crane attached to the front — although never very numerous, have been made for many years. We have several examples in preservation today and it is well worth making the effort to see one. The crane jib is usually detachable, so the engine can appear bereft of this useful fitting.

This photograph shows a Class B6, works number 17212, road engine built by John Fowler & Company (Leeds) Limited in 1929 and delivered new to John Thompson & Company Limited, Boiler Engineers of Wolverhampton, Staffordshire — it still carries their fine brass plate on the motion side cover.

The engine shows all the features of a road engine — large wheels, solid rubber tyres, belly tanks and solid flywheel — the flywheel dished in true Fowler style. The road registration number is R F 6092.

*Overleaf, right:* Travelling showmen and amusement caterers provide facilities for entertainment and relaxation to many people throughout the country; by the very nature of their occupation, the ability to move from place to place has always been of paramount importance to them. So when the traction engine came into being the travelling showman took full advantage of their suitability to his requirements.

Many and various were the road engines used by them and almost all types were used at one time or another.

Engines made by Charles Burrell & Sons Limited were popular with showmen and many were in use by them. This particular engine is number 3118 dating from July 1909 and is generally very similar to the engine number 2824 *Lord Lansdowne* in that both are of 7nhp and spring mounted.

This engine has not always been in showland though, having started its life as an ordinary road haulage engine. Burrell records show it as 'exported to Scotland' where its first owners were McCreath & Co of Berwick. Since then it has had many owners in various parts of the country, 10 being recorded. It was owned and used in showland for many years by the firm of C. W. Abbott of Norwich whose name appears on the cab side boards today; he had it in the early 1920s so it received the appropriate Norfolk registration number, AH 5305.

H.L. CRANE WOLVERHAMPTON
RF 6092

CHAS. ABBOTT & SONS · AMUSEMENTS

S.J.WHARTON FOR MECHANICAL & ELECTRICAL ENGINEERING
KING GEORGE VI

*Left:* Burrell showmans road locomotive No 3489 *King George VI*, registration number PB 9624, built 1916, 6nhp.

*Overleaf, left:* Continuing this brief photographic review of Burrell showland engines, here is a 'Special Scenic' a class of engine specially introduced to cope with the heavy electrical load required to handle the big 'Scenic' rides then being used by showmen. This involved fitting a second dynamo or 'exciter', which on Burrell engines was placed between the chimney and cylinder block and can be clearly seen in this photograph.

Burrell number 3909 is of 8nhp and was built in April 1922. Used in showland for many years by the firm of Holland of Swadlincote, the plate recording this can be clearly seen on the side of the engine. Subsequently the engine moved to Worcestershire where it was owned by Mr Eric Middleton and became a feature of his well-known Hartlebury steam parties in the early days of preservation. It is now in north-east England and appears regularly at rallies.

The water-lift pipe carried on the side of the belly tank is also of note as is the fact that the engine has been generating electricity and the wires are clearly visible leading from the ammeters.

This engine now bears the proud name of *Winston Churchill* and has the Leicestershire road registration number NR 965.

*Overleaf, right:* The name of Aveling and Porter is synonymous with steam road rollers and indeed a photograph of a fine example of such a product is elsewhere in this book. But Avelings built a wide range of traction engines of all types, and quite a few examples of their products other than steam rollers exist today; they are interesting engines and worth looking out for.

This photograph is one of the rarest of Aveling types in existence today — the heavy road locomotive; particularly so in showman form. In the early days up to World War I Avelings built many road locomotives and they were to be seen in large numbers particularly in south-eastern England.

This engine is a big one of massive proportions; some idea of its size can be gauged from the figures at the rear of the engine. It is works number 4885 which left the Rochester, Kent, works in 1901 as an ordinary haulage engine for the Admiralty at Chatham; it is of 8nhp.

After Admiralty ownership it spent most of its working life in Essex, being owned in 1924 by Rusland Limited of Chelmsford. By 1935 it had been acquired by the amusement caterers Charles Presland of Tilbury who added the usual showland fittings. Although not so ornate as some show engines, it bears the name *Samson*. The road registration number is ME 6052.

HOLLAND'S GOLDEN DRAGONS
WINSTON CHURCHILL
ALBERT HOLLAND
SWADLINCOTE

CHARLES PRESLAND. AMUSEMENT CATERER
SAMSON

V. KIRK · GOLDEN GALLOPERS · ON TOUR
QUEEN MARY

*Overleaf, left:* Brown & May Limited, Engineers of Devizes, Wiltshire, are one of the exceptions to most engineering firms connected with agriculture being on the eastern side of England. But nevertheless they are very much in an arable agricultural area.

Originally founded in 1854 they had a long and distinguished output of engines and boilers of all types and a handbill dated 1909 claims 'upwards of 8,000 engines and boilers made' and over 70 awards of medals — some record.

During this long period of manufacture quite a few traction engines were made and steam road engines were also turned out. But few of these machines survive today.

One that does is shown in this picture; a well-restored and well turned out small road engine of 5nhp with the works number 8742. It was new to Mr J. Cooke of North Wales and by 1921 was in the ownership of the Nottingham amusement caterers of Hibble and Mellors who, presumably, converted the engine for showland use adding the usual fittings (the belt driving the dynamo from the flywheel can be seen in the photograph). Not surprisingly it carries the Nottingham road registration number AU 4705.

This size of road engine is sometimes considered rather small, but it is a true road engine and quite a few 5hp road engines exist today.

*Overleaf, right:* Burrell road engines were popular with showmen and many were purchased new for this purpose; whether this was due to the quality of the engine, good salesmanship on the part of Burrells or the leasing and hiring arrangements the manufacturer operated at one time is difficult to say — no doubt each contributed.

Burrell number 3443 is an example of an engine supplied new to showland owners Messrs Anderton and Rowland of Plymouth. Built in February 1913 and of 8nhp it is, in common with most road engines, of three speeds and spring mounted.

The original owners had this engine for many years, probably 30, and it passed from their ownership almost directly into preservation, appearing at some of the earliest rallies.

Anderton and Rowland had many engines in course of time and they must have been good owners from the point of view of care and maintenance, since no less than four of their big showman type road engines are still in existence.

Most showman-owned engines were named, often given imposing or noble titles: number 3443 bears the illustrious name *Lord Nelson* and has the unique distinction of being owned by nobility in the outstanding collection at Beaulieu of Lord Montagu.

JOHN H. RUNDLE & SONS          NEW BOLINGBROKE

NATIONAL MOTOR MUSEUM BEAULIEU
CO 3822
ANDERTON
&
ROWLAND
AMUSEMENT
CATERERS
BRISTOL
ANDERTON & ROWLAND AMUSEMENT CATERERS
TRACTION ENGINE

CF 3355
F. & B. LOBB. SHIPSTON ON STOUR
SPARKLE

*Left:* 1896 Burrell 6nhp (makers number 1945) named *Sparkie* is now preserved.

*Overleaf, left:* Burrell showmans road locomotive number 4000 is the most recent of this type of engine, built by Charles Burrell & Sons Limited illustrated in this book. Supplied new in February 1925 to the order of G. T. Tuby, Amusement Caterer of Doncaster, Yorkshire it is an 8nhp engine of three speeds and is spring mounted and has the Yorkshire (West Riding) road registration number WT 8606.

Of particular interest in this photograph is the top of the crane post appearing above the cab at the rear of the engine; the jib crane which was affixed to this post was used to lift the heavier equipment of the rides used by showmen in conjunction with the wire rope (or winch) which was carried and driven by the engine through its normal shafts with the driving pins removed.

The first owner, Mr G. T. Tuby was a showman who took a keen interest in local politics serving as an alderman and was at one time Mayor of Doncaster. His show engines bear witness to this in their names of *Alderman, Mayor* and *Ex-mayor*, this latter being the only one to survive and is illustrated here. The engine is now in the fine and varied collection of traction engines of Mr W. H. McAlpine.

*Overleaf, right:* Elsewhere in this book is a photograph of Mr Burgess's Burrell roller; here is his fine show engine *Earl Haig* — Mr Burgess is prominent in the traction engine world and the excellence of his engines is well-known.

This Burrell is number 3979 and was built in June 1924 and is of 6nhp. It started life as an ordinary road engine with Messrs W. J. Taylor & Sons of Midsomer Norton, Bath, Somerset, and hence received the Somerset road registration number YA 9138. Later it was bought for use in showland by Mrs Flo Symonds of Gloucester when the appropriate fittings were added. Subsequently it passed through the hands of Messrs F. Darby & Son in the eastern counties — a firm who have handled a great number of engines over the years, many of which are in preservation today.

When a show engine was used on the showground to generate electricity there was always present a fire risk from sparks to the many canvas covered stalls and rides; also there was much less draught available when the engine was not moving. Both of these factors could be helped by the use of a tall 'extension' chimney which can be seen in use in this photograph. At other times this 'extension' chimney was carried on a special rack on the top of the cab.

CHARLES BURRELL & SONS LTD. · ENGINEERS · THETFORD
W18606
EX-MAYOR

STANLEY BURGESS & SONS
draw-a-straw
YA 9138

G.MARSH ENGINEER

*Left:* An example of a Foster steam tractor which is now preserved.

*Overleaf, left:* Few firms that manufactured traction engines have been in existence longer than Ruston & Hornsby Limited of Sheaf Iron Works, Lincoln. They are still in existence and are probably now better known for their excavators and diggers.

In 1840 a Mr Proctor was in business in Lincoln. By 1860 a Mr Ruston had appeared on the scene and the firm was known as Ruston, Proctor & Company. It was in this period that steam engines of all types began to be manufactured in quantity — a catalogue of the early 1900s claims '26,000 steam engines sold and 200 prize medals and awards'. Such was their industry and the quality of their products.

During the course of time their agricultural traction engine was produced in fair numbers along with portable, stationary and railway engines and of course their steam and later oil engine mechanical diggers — many of the steam type being used to dig the Manchester Ship Canal.

With the 1904 Extension of the 1903 Motor Car Act, Ruston, Proctor & Company Limited, produced a small road engine or steam tractor of under 5 tons weight for one man operation. It is said that only between 90 and 100 of these little machines were built — Class SCD and designated by their makers 'Lincoln Imp'.

This one is works number 52573 built to a War Department order in 1918. Subsequently owned by Issac Ball & Sons of Wharles, Preston as a roller and registered in Lancashire as number TF 8240. Now in preservation in its original tractor form.

*Overleaf, right:* William Foster & Company Limited of the Wellington Foundry, Lincoln were another of the many engineering firms to spring up in the eastern counties of England whose activities were mainly to provide and service equipment for the arable farmers.

They were established in 1856 and produced many types of steam engine over the following 100 years or so. The majority of their early production was of stationary engines of all sizes, whilst portables were also turned out.

In the traction engine field, which they concentrated on later than some manufacturers, they produced an excellent range of self-moving engines, their road haulage engines often being rated amongst the best of their types. One such engine, a steam tractor adorned with full showmans fittings is depicted here.

This is an interesting engine having started life in 1910 as a convertible roller; ie an engine which was capable of fairly quick conversion to a tractor by substitution of wheels for rolls and vice versa. Often a convertible was sold with both sets of wheels and rolls.

This tractor has the works number 12509 and is of the 5ton (unladen weight) category. Its first owner was Mr T. Pound of Bewdley and the engine bears the road registration number UX 6727. The showland fittings were added later in its career.

Fosters have the distinction of making what was probably the last commercially produced and used traction engine in 1942.

TF 8240

J. SWINGLER WEST BRIDGFORD NOTTS
JS
MAID MARIAN

TIGER
4662

*Left:* A 1918 Fowler 'Tiger' Type T3 tractor No 14412 of 4nhp.

*Overleaf, left:* Garretts of Leiston (Suffolk) or more properly Richard Garrett & Sons were in business in this small Suffolk town not far from Aldeburgh for over 180 years. During this time a vast range of products were turned out, the majority of them for agriculture. Latterly much of their production was devoted to road vehicles using different types of propulsion.

Many types of steam engine were produced but by far the most common seen on the rally field today is the 5ton tractor. These sturdy and economical little machines were built to take advantage of the provisions of the Motor Car Act 1903, being first produced by the company in 1905 and continuing until almost 1930.

The example shown here is a good representative of the Garrett steam tractor. This particular one which is adorned with the showland fittings of long cab, twisted brass and dynamo, did not see use by a showman but had these added in preservation days. Garrett works number 33545 is however an interesting engine having been used for very many years commercially by the transport contractor Messrs J. Harkness & Company in Belfast. It was still in use in the 1950s and was subsequently brought back to this country for preservation.

In common with many steam motor tractors it was first registered by the manufacturer and this one has the East Suffolk registration number BJ 4384.

*Overleaf, right:* Ransomes, Sims & Jefferies Limited, of Orwell Works, Ipswich, were connected with agricultural and road transport products for very many years. With the 1904 extension to the 1903 Motor Car Act it could be expected that they would produce their version of the light road engine, and so they did.

Most readers would be excused for thinking that the little engine in this photograph is one of them; but this would only be partially correct as, strictly speaking, it is an agricultural tractor or ploughing engine — but direct traction ploughing, not cable ploughing as in the more conventional steam ploughing engine.

The system of pulling a plough through the ground with a power unit has been, and still is, the conventional system. So the steam traction engine was tried as a power unit; in some parts of the world where grain is grown over vast areas, direct traction steam ploughing was popular with large engines hauling ploughs producing as many as 20 furrows at a time.

The small steam tractor was tried in this country and although quite successful was really too late and too heavy to combat the challenge of the internal combustion engined tractor.

The Ransome agricultural tractor shown here is a typical agricultural engine with spoked flywheel, iron wheels and is without motion covers. It is works number 39149, built in 1928 and new to Mr E. Johnson of Offchurch, Warwickshire. The road registration number is VE 7213.

PRIDE OF SURREY
BJ 4384
DAVID LAILEY & SON
BARRETT

RANSOMES.

A.C.NAPPER MEADOW HOUSE APPLEFORD BERKS
TIGER
SP 8063

*Left:* This Fowler 'Tiger' type steam tractor was built in 1920 and typical of its make and era.

*Overleaf, left:* Elsewhere in this book is a photograph of a Tasker roller No 1409 with a brief note of this maker's excellent small road engine or tractor. This small engine continued to be made until the late 1920s and this photograph shows the tractor version, which is a neat and workmanlike job.

Built in 1928 and bearing the works number 1928 (surely a coincidence) this little engine originally had the road registration number TK 1440, but has now acquired the later registration of number 932 CRO. The first owner was Mr E. R. Debenham of Briantspuddle, Dorset — hence the Dorset registration. Later it came into the North London area and had several owners before being purchased for preservation by Mr Francis Grover of Amersham.

This was appropriate since Mr Grover had owned a number of Tasker tractors in his timber hauling business and he has also the timber trailer which appears in the photograph complete with load.

Both this Tasker 5ton tractor and the other Tasker roller are of makers Class B2 and have compound cylinders with overhead valves. Of particular interest is the final drive of this engine which is by chain which can just be seen behind the rear wheel.

*Overleaf, right:* Here is a further example of the varied types of self-propelled steam engine manufactured by Marshall, Sons & Company Limited of Gainsborough; this one of the rarer types from this firm — a steam tractor. Although many Marshall engines are in existence to this day, there are not many tractors.

Built in 1920 and delivered new to Norfolk County Council, number 73900 received the road registration appropriate to the county, number AH 823 (originally AH 0823; Norfolk was the only county to use 'O' as a prefix to the actual number; this still appears on some engines to this day).

The engine did not stay long in Norfolk as by 1923 it was reported in ownership in Surrey. It is still south of London and has had several owners up to the present time.

In common with almost all tractors it is a compound engine, in this case with slide valves on the side and is classified as of 5tons unladen weight to keep within the requirements of the 1904 extension of the 1903 Motor Car Act which amongst other things allowed a higher speed and one-man operation.

Note also the fine brass lamps carried each side of the smokebox.

932 CRO

AH 823

D.C. HACKETT          BRIDSTOW          ROSS - ON - WYE

*Left:* Aveling & Porter tractor No 9225. Registration number CJ 4160, built 1920, photographed at Bishop's Castle in 1970.

*Overleaf, left:* There are three colour photographs of products of the Rochester Works of Aveling & Porter Limited in this book; each one of a different class of engine which is fortunate.

This photograph is of the Aveling version of the steam motor tractor built to comply with the provisions of the 1904 Extension Order of the 1903 Motor Car Act. There are many of these little Aveling engines in preservation; they are attractive little machines that merit some study.

The order permitted an engine to haul a load on the highway at 5mph and to be crewed by one man, only provided it weighed less than 5 tons: so almost all traction engine makers turned out these small road locomotives known as steam tractors.

They had all the features of their larger brothers — solid flywheel and plates covering the 'motion' or moving parts of the engine, both features said to have been introduced on road engines to prevent horses taking fright; extra water tanks, or belly tanks — quite large in this instance — to give a greater range between water pick-ups with solid rubber tyres on the wheels and a compound engine in this instance with piston valves clearly seen on the outside of the cylinders.

Works number 11486 was new in 1926 to the Kent County Council and is of makers Class L. It carries the road registration number KM 7100 and the name *Anne Marie*.

*Overleaf, right:* The Sentinel Waggon Works Limited introduced a type known as the Super Sentinel in 1923. This manufacturer had remained faithful to the vertical boiler and their products were popular; but with the 'Super' range they produced a wagon which was much improved over existing types both with conventional locomotive type boilers and vertical water tube boilers.

Towards the end of the 1920s a new and improved type known as the DG was introduced (DG standing for Double Geared). These Sentinel types are worth studying as they incorporate some interesting features. The boiler and the engine are separated from each other. The boiler is beside the driver who sits right forward with the controls with an excellent view of the road and of the gauges etc, on the boiler which is fed from the top — the mate sits level with the driver and can attend to the boiler. The engine is horizontal and placed between or under the chassis, thereby allowing a long and uninterrupted platform for load carrying.

This photograph shows a DG type wagon, in the six wheel version, and is makers number 8590, and was built in 1931. It was new to the Cement Marketing Company of London, hence the London registration number GT 2827.

KM 7100

SENTINEL
STEAM WAGGON
BUILT 1931
SPEED - 20 MPH
GT 2827

STAR OF ACRISE
G. Marsh
ACRISE
Foden
YKE 666H

*Left:* Foden wagon No 11892 *Star of Acrise*, registration number VKE 666H. Built 1927, photographed at Acrise in 1970.

*Overleaf, left:* Steam wagons were in use on the roads in this country for just over half a century; two distinct types were met — the undertype of which there are four photographs elsewhere in this book, and the overtype.

The overtype had the engine 'over' the boiler which was invariably of the locomotive type; thus the overtype could be said to be on traction engine lines whereas the undertype definitely was not. Probably numerically the numbers were about equally divided.

The firm of Fodens of Sandbach near Crewe were to the overtype what Sentinels were to the undertype. The products of Elsworth Works, Sandbach, were more numerous than any other type of steam wagon and were excellent wagons in every respect and many examples of their products are in existence today.

Their first overtype steam wagons were made in 1901 and were successful in the War Office Trials at Aldershot in that year. The general design had been laid-down and by 1910 was much in its final form. Continuous development took place introducing every refinement possible through a range of wagons from three to six tons.

This photograph shows a late type, 6ton standard wagon made in 1929 with the works number 13488. New to the Sun Flour Mills of Bromley-by-Bow, it carried the London road registration number UV 8895. Later it was owned by East and Son, of Berkhamstead and then by Taroads Limited who re-registered it as number RO 6330 when it was in use as a tar tanker. Note the brass plates on the smokebox and the Royal Letters Patent insignia on the chimney.

*Overleaf, right:* Although steam wagons were made and used in this country over the general period 1900 to 1950, few manufacturers produced wagons over the entire period. One such was the Sentinel Waggon Works Limited of Shrewsbury (earlier of Glasgow) who made their first wagon in 1906 and their last in the very early 1950s.

During this long period the general concept of their products remained much the same, with a vertical water tube boiler, superheating of steam, underfloor engine remote from the boiler with forward control position for the crew. The types were few in number — Standard, Super, DG and last of all the 'S' type. With the exception of the last type a twin cylinder duplex engine had been used with final drive to the rear axle by chain.

The 'S' type was their culminating design and was probably the most advanced steam wagon design ever seen. Had penalising taxation and the advance of the diesel engine not driven them off the road, it is interesting to consider how the design might have developed. The main departure from the earlier Sentinel types was the introduction of a four-in-line engine — single acting with the final drive by cardan shaft; the boiler had also been moved to behind the driver.

This photograph shows works number 9003 of February 1934 made for Foster Mills of Cambridge with the road registration number VE 9963. Later it was owned by Spillers (Home Pride Flour).

RO 6330
Foden
TREGUNTER
HAULAGE COY
LONDON S.W.2

4
Spillers
SPILLERS L?
FOSTER MILLS
CAMBRIDGE
TELEPHONE
50251
CAMBRIDGE
SPILLERS
FLOUR MILLERS
SPILLERS·· ·THE·· ·MILLERS
Sentinel

*Overleaf, left:* Steam wagons were once numerous on the roads and handled a great deal of the heavy traffic. The introduction of taxation taking weight into account put the steam wagon with its heavy boiler, engine and water supply at a disadvantage and they gradually disappeared from the commercial scene. Fortunately many are in preservation today, so that examples of the products of most manufacturers can be seen and studied.

In the early days of steam wagons, examples using upright or vertical boilers with water in the tubes were common (there is a photograph of an early Thorneycroft wagon in this book). Later the more tried and economic locomotive type boiler was almost universally adopted.

But one maker remained faithful to the vertical boiler (with the exception of one type) throughout their long and distinguished period of manufacture of steam wagons — these were Sentinels. Alley & McLellan of Glasgow made their first steam wagon in 1906. About 1917 a new Sentinel works was opened at Shrewsbury under the general name of 'Sentinel Waggon Works Limited' — this company used the curious spelling 'waggon' throughout.

This photograph shows one of their excellent DG range of wagons, works number 8571, made in 1931 and bearing the road registration number KF 6482. It was new to Sam Banner Oil Refineries Limited, Liverpool and was later in the ownership of Paul Bros Limited in whose colours it is restored. Note the Sentinel makers plate just above the '6' on the front apron.

*Overleaf, right:* Mann's Patent Steam Cart and Wagon Company Limited of Pepper Road Works, Hunslet, Leeds, were one of the smaller steam engine manufacturers in that illustrious company of traction engine builders at Leeds. Few of their products exist today, but if you come across one it is well worth study as they have some very unusual features.

As their name suggests the majority of their products were for transport, either as tractors or load carrying vehicles together with an interesting light steam roller, at least one example of which is extant today.

The illustration here is of a 5ton wagon with box body bearing the name on the side of the engine of S. E. Frampton, Farnham, one of its earlier owners. The makers number is 1120 and it was made in 1916. A feature of Mann wagons is the driver's position beside the boiler and motion instead of behind as is usual with overtype steam wagons (ie those with a locomotive type boiler with the cylinders and motion 'over' the boiler). The coal is in front of the driver and the firehole door is in the side of the firebox; one man thus drove and steered the vehicle.

Being a road vehicle it was registered under the 1904 Extension Order and as was customary in those days this road registration was done in the county borough of manufacture — hence the Leeds number U 3781.

PAUL BROS LTD
HOMEPRIDE FLOUR MILLS
BIRKENHEAD
6
KF 6482
PAUL BROS LTD HOMEPRIDE FLOUR MILLS BIRKENHEAD
JOHN HOLMAN LTD (CONTRACTORS)

S.F. FRAMPTON
FARNHAM
U-3781

R.BRAZIL & CºLTD
BUILDING CONTRACTORS
AMERSHAM 98

*Left:* A 1928 Foden steam tractor used by building contractors, but also often used for timber haulage and forestry work. This example was preserved and rebuilt in 1963.

*Overleaf:* Many of the early steam wagons built about the turn of the century and just after were undertype wagons, ie in which the cylinders and motion are 'under' the boiler. Usually these were remote from the boiler and were often horizontal and between the chassis or frame members.

The Thorneycroft Steam Wagon Company Limited (John I. Thorneycroft & Company Limited) of Chiswick, London, and Basingstoke were amongst the earliest of steam wagon manufacturers — no doubt as a sideline to their better known marine activities. They were building wagons by 1897 and continued in this line for a relatively short time, probably only about 10 years.

Three sets of trials for road wagons were held in the very early days which were known as the Liverpool Trials of 1898, 1899 and 1901. Messrs Thorneycroft entered their vehicles in all three and achieved some success being awarded medals in all three.

Very few of these very early steam wagons are in existence today, but the photograph shows one that has survived. Thorneycroft number 39 was built in 1900. Its first owner was Mr F. Wintle of Mitcheldean, Gloucestershire and hence it carries a Gloucester road registration number AD 115. It bears the name *Dorothy*. It has a brewers dray body generally similar to a style often encountered in those early days.

PHIPPS BREWERY LIMITED
BRIDGE STREET
NORTHAMPTON
NOTED ALES & BOTTLED STOUTS
DOROTHY
ROBERT H. CRAWFORD & SON